THE LITTLE RED BOOK OF

TEACHER'S WISDOM

THE LITTLE RED BOOK OF
TEACHER'S WISDOM

Edited by Diane Hodges

Skyhorse Publishing

Skyhorse Publishing books may be purchased in bulk at special discounts for sales promotion, corporate gifts, fund-raising, or educational purposes. Special editions can also be created to specifications. For details, contact the Special Sales Department, Skyhorse Publishing, 307 West 36th Street, 11th Floor, New York, NY 10018 or info@skyhorsepublishing.com.

Skyhorse® and Skyhorse Publishing® are registered trademarks of Skyhorse Publishing, Inc.®, a Delaware corporation.

Visit our website at www.skyhorsepublishing.com.

10 9 8 7 6 5 4 3 2 1

Library of Congress Cataloging-in-Publication Data is available on file.

Hardcover ISBN: 978-1-61608-607-7
Paperback ISBN: 978-1-5107-6769-0
Ebook ISBN: 978-1-62087-280-2

Images courtesy of Shutterstock.com

Publisher's Note: While Skyhorse Publishing normally strives for inclusive language in referring to a person of nonspecified gender, the quotes in this book date back to older times and other cultures.

Printed in China

Contents

Introduction

I am addicted to quotes. I love quotes. I collect quotes. I have an entire file cabinet that holds them, and I have moved that cabinet to three different states over the years. As I go toward the end of my career and my life, I envision my children recycling thousands of pages in this quotes cabinet into the recycling bin. To make sure this doesn't occur, I decided to share my file cabinet with you. I put quotes on memos, on bulletin boards, on paychecks, in restrooms . . . anywhere that I know they will be seen. I hope you will, too.

—**Diane Hodges**

PART ONE

Education

There is no word in the language I revere more than "teacher." My heart sings when a kid refers to me as his teacher, and it always has. I've honored myself and the entire family of man by becoming a teacher.
—PAT CONROY

• • •

Children need all school workers. A person is not "just" a janitor, not "just" a custodian. Janitors can see children when (teachers) don't see them, and bus drivers recognize that children who are disruptive on the bus are likely disorderly in the classroom. They're partners in education. We need each other to make this work.
—REV. JESSE JACKSON

• • •

I dedicate myself to the life of an educator, to laying the living foundations upon which successor generations must continue to build their lives.

I dedicate myself to the advancement of learning, for I know that without it our successors will lack both the vision and the power to build well.

I dedicate myself to the cultivation of character, for I know that humanity cannot flourish without courage, compassion, honesty, and trust.

I commit myself to advancement of my own learning and to the cultivation of my own character, for I know that I must bear witness in my own life to the ideals that I have dedicated myself to promote in others.

In the presence of this gathering, I so dedicate and commit myself.

—STEVEN TIGNER, AFFIRMED ANNUALLY IN THE BOSTON UNIVERSITY SCHOOL OF EDUCATION JUNIOR PINNING CEREMONY

• • •

Education

A teacher affects eternity; he can never tell where his influence
stops.
—HENRY B. ADAMS

• • •

It takes a special person with patience and wisdom to share, to
unlock the treasure waiting within children everywhere.
—JOAN ZATORSKI

• • •

The future of the world is in my classroom today, a future with
the potential for good or bad . . . Several future presidents are
learning from me today; so are the great writers of the next
decades, and so are all the so-called ordinary people who will
make decisions in a democracy. I must never forget these
same young people could be the thieves and murderers of
the future. Only a teacher? Thank God I have a calling to the
greatest profession of all! I must be vigilant every day, lest I
lose one fragile opportunity to improve tomorrow.

—IVAN WELTON FITZWATER

• • •

One looks back with appreciation to the brilliant teachers, but with gratitude to those who touched our human feeling. The curriculum is so much necessary raw material, but warmth is the vital element for the growing plan and for the soul of the child.
—CARL JUNG

• • •

Teachers can change lives with just the right mix of chalk and challenges.
—JOYCE A. MYERS

• • •

I like to think that the greatest success of any life is the moment when a teacher touches a child's heart and it is never again the same . . . Everything America is or ever hopes to be depends upon what happens in our school's classrooms.
—FROSTY TROY

• • •

Any teacher can study books, but books do not necessarily bring wisdom, nor that human insight essential to consummate teaching skills.
—BLISS PERRY

• • •

One never notices what has been done;
one can only see what remains to be done.
—MARIE CURIE

• • •

A teacher is like a candle which lights others in consuming itself.
—GIOVANNI RUFFINI

• • •

What the teacher is, is more important than what he teaches.

—KARL MENNINGER

• • •

Teachers know there will always be rocks in the road ahead of us. They will be stumbling blocks or stepping stones; it all depends on how we use them.
—UNKNOWN

• • •

Better than a thousand days of diligent study is one day with a great teacher.
—JAPANESE PROVERB

• • •

A teacher's constant task is to take a roomful of live wires and see to it that they're grounded.
—E.C. MCKENZIE

• • •

It is noble to teach oneself, but still nobler to teach others—
and less trouble.
—MARK TWAIN

• • •

One hundred years from now it will not matter what my bank
account was, the type of house I lived in, or the kind of car I
drove, but the world may be different because I was important
in the life of a child.
—FOREST WITCRAFT, EXCERPT FROM
"WITHIN MY POWER"

• • •

To live a single day and hear a good teaching is better than to
live a hundred years without knowing such teaching.
—BUDDHA

• • •

A teacher who can arouse a feeling for one single good action, for one single good poem, accomplishes more than he who fills our memory with rows and rows of natural objects, classified with name and form.
—JOHANN WOLFGANG VON GOETHE

• • •

In a completely rational society, the best of us would be teachers and the rest of us would have to settle for something less because passing civilization along from one generation to the next ought to be the highest honor and responsibility anyone can have.
—LEE IACOCCA

• • •

A great teacher never strives to explain his vision. He simply invites you to stand beside himself and see for yourself.
—R. INNAN

• • •

I've always tried to be aware of what I say in my films, because all of us who make motion pictures are teachers—teachers with very loud voices.
—GEORGE LUCAS

• • •

Compassionate teachers fill a void left by working parents who aren't able to devote enough attention to their children. Teachers don't just teach; they can be vital personalities who help young people to mature, to understand the world and to understand themselves. A good education consists of much more than useful facts and marketable skills.
—CHARLES PLATT

• • •

Teachers, I believe, are the most responsible and important members of society because their professional efforts affect the fate of the earth.
—HELEN CALDICOTT

• • •

I put the relation of a fine teacher to a student just below the
relation of a mother to a son . . .
—THOMAS WOLFE

• • •

Teachers are the reservoirs from which, through the process
of education, students draw the water of life.
—SRI SATHYA SAI BABA

• • •

A good teacher, like a good entertainer, first must hold his
audience's attention. Then he can teach his lesson.
—HENDRIK JOHN CLARKE

• • •

What sculpture is to a block of marble, education is to the
soul.
—JOSEPH ADDISON

• • •

Teachers teach because they care. Teaching young people is
what they do best. It requires long hours, patience, and care.
—HORACE MANN

• • •

Teachers are expected to reach unattainable goals with inad-
equate tools. The miracle is that at times they accomplish this
impossible task.
—HAIM G. GINOTT

• • •

Teachers who inspire know that teaching is like cultivating a garden, and those who would have nothing to do with thorns must never attempt to gather flowers.
—UNKNOWN

• • •

Whoever first coined the phrase "you're the wind beneath my wings" most assuredly was reflecting on the sublime influence of a very special teacher.
—FRANK TRUJILLO

• • •

What greater or better gift can we offer the republic than to teach and instruct our youth.
—MARCUS TULLIUS CICERO

• • •

What a teacher doesn't say is a telling part of what a student hears.
—MAURICE NATANSON

• • •

You can pay people to teach, but you can't pay them to care.
—MARVA COLLINS

• • •

The dream begins, most of the time, with a teacher who believes in you, who tugs and pushes and leads you onto the next plateau, sometimes poking you with a sharp stick called truth.
—DAN RATHER

• • •

If a man keeps cherishing his old knowledge, so as to continu-
ingly be acquiring new, he may be a teacher of others.
—CONFUCIUS

• • •

A loving heart is the beginning of all knowledge.
—THOMAS CARLYLE

• • •

He who dares to teach must never cease to learn.
—RICHARD HENRY DANN

• • •

We cannot hold a torch to light another's path without bright-
ening our own.
—BEN SWEETLAND

• • •

Education is light; lack of it is darkness.
—RUSSIAN PROVERB

• • •

There is a place in America to take a stand: it is public education. It is the underpinning of our cultural and political system. It is the great common ground. Public education after all is the engine that moves us as a society toward a common destiny . . . it is in public education that the American dream begins to take shape.
—TOM BROKAW

• • •

Schools will change more in the next 30 years than they have since the invention of the printed book.
—PETER DRUCKER

• • •

We can talk or dream about the glorious schools of the future
or we can create them.
—MARILYN FERGUSON

• • •

Knowledge changes extremely fast. But that in itself is not
new; knowledge has always been fast. What is new is that
knowledge matters.
—PETER DRUCKER

• • •

Education is the most important profession because through
the hands of educators pass all professions.
—UNKNOWN

• • •

The most important outcome of education is to help students become independent of formal education.
—PAUL E. GRAY

• • •

Education could be much more effective if its purpose was to ensure that by the time they leave school every boy and girl should know how much they do not know, and be imbued with a lifelong desire to know it.
—WILLIAM HALEY

• • •

Education's purpose is to replace an empty mind with an open one.
—MALCOLM S. FORBES

• • •

For the first time in human history it really matters whether or not people learn.
—PETER DRUCKER

• • •

Education that consists of learning things and not the meaning of them is feeding upon husks and not corn.
—MARK TWAIN

• • •

There is an old saying that the course of civilization is a race between catastrophe and education. In a democracy such as ours, we must make sure that education wins the race.
—JOHN F. KENNEDY

• • •

We cannot always build the future for our youth, but we can build our youth for the future.
—FRANKLIN D. ROOSEVELT

• • •

Every time you stop a school, you will have to build a jail. What you gain at one end, you lose at the other. It's like feeding a dog on his own tail. It won't fatten the dog.
—MARK TWAIN

• • •

There is only one thing that costs more than education today—the lack of it.
—UNKNOWN

• • •

Education today, more than ever before, must see clearly the dual objectives: education for living and education for making a living.
—JAMES MASON WOOD

• • •

The goal of formal education has always been to produce people who could continue to learn on their own.
—RONALD GROSS

• • •

The highest result of education is tolerance.
—HELEN KELLER

• • •

Education is the ability to listen to almost anything without losing your temper.
—ROBERT FROST

• • •

Thinking is the hardest work there is, which is the probable reason why so few engage in it.
—HENRY FORD

• • •

Education is the key to unlock the golden door of freedom.
—GEORGE WASHINGTON CARVER

• • •

Education is a better safeguard of liberty than a standing
army.
—EDWARD EVERETT

• • •

Without education, you're not going anywhere in this world.
—MALCOLM X

• • •

Genius without education is like silver in the mine.
—BENJAMIN FRANKLIN

• • •

Education is the movement from darkness to light.
—ALLAN BLOOM

• • •

We are now at a point where we must educate our children in what no one knew yesterday, and prepare our schools for what no one knows yet.
—MARGARET MEAD

• • •

If a man empties his purse into his head, no man can take it from him. An investment in knowledge always pays the best interest.
—BENJAMIN FRANKLIN

• • •

Upon the subject of education, not presuming to dictate any plan or system respecting it, I can only say that I view it as the most important subject we as people may be engaged in.
—ABRAHAM LINCOLN

• • •

The most important thing about education is appetite.
—WINSTON CHURCHILL

• • •

The education of a man is never complete until he dies.
—ROBERT E. LEE

• • •

Education is what survives when what has been learned has been forgotten.
—B.F. SKINNER

• • •

Investment in a human soul? Who knows? It might be a diamond in the rough.
—MARY MCLEOD BETHUNE

• • •

The end of all education should surely be service to others.
—CESAR CHAVEZ

• • •

Education is simply the soul of a society as it passes from one generation to another.
—G.K. CHESTERTON

• • •

When I was a boy on the Mississippi River there was a proposition in a township there to discontinue public schools because they were too expensive. An old farmer spoke up and said if they stopped building the schools they would not save anything, because every time a school was closed a jail had to be built.
—MARK TWAIN

• • •

Knowledge exists to be imparted.
—RALPH WALDO EMERSON

• • •

Education is for improving the lives of others and for leaving
your community and world better than you found it.
—MARIAN WRIGHT EDELMAN

• • •

It is possible to store the mind with a million facts and still be
entirely uneducated.
—ALLAN BLOOM

• • •

Upon the education of the people of this country the fate of
the country depends.
—BENJAMIN DISRAELI

• • •

Education is too important to be left solely to the educators.
—FRANCIS KEPPEL

• • •

If you want years of prosperity, grow grain.
If you want ten years of prosperity, grow trees.
If you want one hundred years of prosperity, grow people.
—CHINESE PROVERB

• • •

The great aim of education is not knowledge but action.
—HERBERT SPENCER

• • •

It is not the IQ but the I WILL that is the most important in education.
—UNKNOWN

• • •

The direction in which education starts a man will
determine his future.
—PLATO

• • •

Education is a vaccine for violence.
—EDWARD JAMES OLMOS

• • •

Education is the ability to meet life's situation.
—JOHN G. HIBBEN

• • •

Only the educated are free.
—EPICTETUS

• • •

Wisdom is one treasure that no thief can touch.
—JAPANESE PROVERB

• • •

If I were to enumerate ten educational stupidities, the giving of grades would head the list . . . If I can't give a child a better reason for studying than a grade on a report card, I ought to lock my desk and go home and stay there.
—DOROTHY DE ZOUCHE

• • •

Our progress as a nation can be no swifter than our progress in education. The human mind is our fundamental resource.
—JOHN F. KENNEDY

• • •

Education costs money, but then so does ignorance.
—CLAUS MOSER

• • •

Creating schools for the 21st century requires less time looking in the rear view mirror and more vision anticipating the road ahead.
—GEORGE LUCAS

• • •

When making a decision, ask the question "Is it good for kids?" If the response is "yes," then you have your answer.
—DIANE HODGES

• • •

Much that passes for education is not education at all
but ritual. The fact is that we are being educated when we
know it least.
—DAVID P. GARDNER

• • •

Knowledge—like the sky—is never private property . . .
teaching is the art of sharing.
—ABRAHAM JOSHUA HESCHEL

• • •

It is the supreme art of the teacher to awaken joy in creative
expression and knowledge.
—ALBERT EINSTEIN

• • •

Let us think of education as the means of developing our greatest abilities, because in each of us there is a private hope and dream which, fulfilled, can be translated into benefit for everyone and greater strength for our nation.
—JOHN F. KENNEDY

• • •

The whole art of teaching is only the art of awakening the natural curiosity of young minds for the purpose of satisfying it afterwards.
—ANATOLE FRANCE

• • •

The job of the teacher is to teach students to see the viability in themselves.
—JOSEPH CAMPBELL

• • •

In teaching children we must seek insensibly to unite knowledge with the carrying out of that knowledge into practice.
—IMMANUEL KANT

• • •

The art of teaching is the art of assisting discovery.
—MARK VAN DOREN

• • •

Education to be successful must not only inform but inspire.
—T. SHARPER KNOWLSON

• • •

Real education should consist of drawing the goodness and the best out of our own students. What better books can there be than the book of humanity?
—CESAR CHAVEZ

• • •

Teach others NOT what you have learned, BUT what you are learning.
—CRAIG PACE

• • •

I teach with my heart and soul and not with my mouth alone.
—JAIME ESCALANTE

• • •

Be all that you can be. Find your future—as a teacher.
—MADELINE FUCHS HOLZER

• • •

The mediocre teacher tells. The good teacher explains. The superior teacher demonstrates. The great teacher inspires.
—WILLIAM ARTHUR WARD

• • •

It's never enough to just tell people about some new insight. Rather, you have to get them to experience it in a way that evokes its power and possibility. Instead of pouring knowledge into people's hands, you need to help them grind a new set of eyeglasses so they can see the world in a new way.
—JOHN SEELY BROWN

• • •

I care not what subject is taught, if only it be taught well.
—T.H. HUXLEY

• • •

The object of teaching a child is to enable him to get along without his teacher.
—ELBERT HUBBARD

• • •

Treat a man as he is and he will remain as he is. Treat a man as he can and should be and he will become as he can and should be.
—JOHANN WOLFGANG VON GOETHE

• • •

The secret of teaching is to appear as to have known all your life what you learned this afternoon.
—UNKNOWN

• • •

Spoon feeding in the long run teaches us nothing but the shape of the spoon.
—E.M. FORSTER

• • •

In seeking knowledge, the first step is silence, the second listening, the third remembering, the fourth practicing, and the fifth—teaching others.
—SOLOMON IBN GABIROL

• • •

A teacher's day is one-half bureaucracy, one-half crisis, one-half monotony, and one-eighth epiphany. Never mind the arithmetic.
—SUSAN OHANIAN

• • •

Good teachers never say anything. What they do is create the conditions under which learning takes place.
—S.I. HAYAKAWA

• • •

Education is not filling a bucket but lighting a fire.
—WILLIAM BUTLER YEATS

• • •

Children have to be educated, but they also have to be left to educate themselves.
—ERNEST DIMNET

• • •

If a child can't learn the way we teach, maybe we should teach the way they learn.
—IGNACIO ESTRADA

• • •

The most important thing is not so much that every child should be taught, as that every child should be given the wish to learn.
—JOHN LUBBOCK

• • •

Those who educate children well are to be honored more than parents, for these only gave life, and teachers the art of living well.
—ARISTOTLE

• • •

Do not train a child to learn by force or harshness; but direct them to it by what amuses their minds, so that you may be better able to discover with accuracy the peculiar bent of the genius of each.
—PLATO

• • •

The best teachers teach from the heart, not from the book.
—UNKNOWN

• • •

I do not teach. I relate.
—MICHEL DE MONTAIGNE

• • •

Example isn't another way to teach, it is the only way to teach.
—ALBERT EINSTEIN

• • •

How to tell students what to look for without telling them
what to see is the dilemma of teaching.
—LASCELLES ABERCROMBIE

• • •

The beauty of empowering others is that your own power is
not diminished in the process.
—BARBARA COLOROSE

• • •

If a doctor, lawyer, or dentist had forty people in his office at one time, all of whom had different needs, and some of whom didn't want to be there and were causing trouble, and the doctor, lawyer, or dentist, without assistance, had to treat them all with professional excellence for nine months, then he might have some conception of the classroom teacher's job.
—DONALD D. QUINN

• • •

Good teaching is one-fourth preparation and three-fourths theater.
—GAIL GODWIN

• • •

A teacher is one who makes himself progressively unnecessary.
—THOMAS CARRUTHERS

• • •

Don't try to fix the students, fix ourselves first. The good teacher makes the poor student good and the good student superior. When our students fail, we, as teachers, too, have failed.
—MARVA COLLINS

• • •

I like the teacher that gives you something to take home to think about besides homework.
—LILY TOMLIN AS "EDITH ANN"

• • •

In teaching you cannot see the fruit of a day's work. It is invisible and remains so, maybe for twenty years.
—JACQUE BARZUN

• • •

You cannot teach a man anything; you can only help him find it within himself.
—GALILEO

• • •

Teaching was the hardest work I have ever done . . .
—ANN RICHARDS

• • •

Too often we give our children answers to remember rather than problems to solve.
—ROGER LEWIN

• • •

Teach to the problems, not to the text.
—E. KIM NEBEUTS

• • •

Teachers open the door, but you must enter by yourself.
—CHINESE PROVERB

• • •

Minds are like parachutes—they only function when open.
—THOMAS DEWAR

• • •

Learning is by nature curiosity.
—PLATO

• • •

Free the child's potential, and you will transform him into
the world.
—MARIA MONTESSORI

• • •

Human beings strive for understanding and mastery, and tend to be motivated when they effectively learn something they value.
—RAYMOND WLODKOWSKI

• • •

The mind is not a vessel to be filled, but a fire to be ignited.
—PLATO

• • •

When you are through learning, you're through.
—VERNON LAW

• • •

The most beautiful thing about learning is that no one can take it away from you.
—B.B. KING

• • •

Live as if you were to die tomorrow. Learn as if you were to live forever.
—MAHATMA GANDHI

• • •

He who would learn to fly one day must first learn to stand and walk and run and climb and dance; one cannot fly into flying.
—FRIEDRICH NIETZSCHE

• • •

I hear, and I forget. I see, and I remember. I do, and I understand.
—CHINESE PROVERB

• • •

I forget what I was taught. I only remember what I have learned.
—PATRICK WHITE

• • •

The focus of learning will shift from schools to employers.
—PETER DRUCKER

• • •

Learning is finding out what you already known,
Doing is demonstrating that you know it,
Teaching is reminding others that you know it
as well as you do.
We are all learners, doers, and teachers.
—RICHARD BACH

• • •

Life does not consist mainly, or even largely, of facts and
happenings. It consists mainly of the storm of thought that is
forever flowing through one's head.
—MARK TWAIN

• • •

Experience is a hard teacher because she gives the test first,
and the lesson afterward.
—VERNON LAW

• • •

Man's mind, once stretched by a new idea, never again regains
its original dimensions.
—OLIVER WENDELL HOLMES

• • •

Never stop learning; knowledge doubles every fourteen
months.
—ANTHONY J. D'ANGELO

• • •

Invest in yourself, in your education. There's nothing better.
—SYLVIA PORTER

• • •

Not I, but the city teaches.
—SOCRATES

• • •

Where did we ever get the crazy idea that in order to make people do better, first we must make them feel worse? Think of the last time you felt humiliated or treated unfairly. Did you feel like cooperating or doing better?
—JANE NELSON

• • •

The most effective kind of education is that a child should play amongst lovely things.
—UNKNOWN

• • •

Today a reader, tomorrow a leader.
—MARGARET FULLER

• • •

Think left and think right and think low and think high. Oh,
the thinks you can think up if only you try!
—DR. SEUSS

• • •

There is more treasure in books than in all the pirates' loot on
Treasure Island.
—WALT DISNEY

• • •

Nature and books belong to the eyes that see them.
—RALPH WALDO EMERSON

• • •

To learn to read is to light a fire; every syllable that is spelled
out is a spark.
—VICTOR HUGO

• • •

The more that you read, the more things that you will know.
The more that you learn, the more places you'll go.
—DR. SEUSS

• • •

America's future walks through the doors of our schools
every day.
—MARY JEAN LETENDRE

• • •

Students are volunteers, whether we want them to be or not.
Their attendance can be commanded, but their attention must
be earned. Their compliance can be insisted upon, but their
commitment is under their own control.
—PHILIP SCHLECHTY

• • •

I consider a human soul without education like marble in a
quarry, which shows none of its inherent beauties until the
skill of the polisher sketches out the colors, makes the surface
shine, and discovers every ornamental cloud, spot, and vein
that runs through it.
—JOSEPH ADDISON

• • •

There is a brilliant child locked inside every student.
—MARVA COLLINS

• • •

We worry about what a child will become tomorrow, yet we
forget that he is someone today.
—STACIA TAUSCHER

• • •

Every child is born a genius.
—ALBERT EINSTEIN

• • •

A child miseducated is a child lost.
—JOHN F. KENNEDY

• • •

All children have creative power.
—BRENDA UELAND

• • •

It is important that students bring a certain ragamuffin, bare-foot irreverence to their studies; they are not here to worship what is known, but to question it.
—JACOB BRONOWSKI

• • •

Everyone is ignorant, only on different subjects.
—WILL ROGERS

• • •

It is not the strongest of the species that survives, not the most intelligent, but the most responsive to change.
—CHARLES DARWIN

• • •

The only person who is educated is the one who has learned how to learn and change.
—CARL ROGERS

• • •

PART TWO

Children

Your children are not your children.
They are the sons and daughters of Life's longing for itself . . .
You may house their bodies but not their souls,
For their souls dwell in the house of tomorrow,
Which you cannot visit, not even in your dreams.
—KAHLIL GIBRAN

• • •

Let us put our minds together and see what life we can make
for our children.
—SITTING BULL

• • •

Children are one-third of our population and all of our future.
—SELECT PANEL FOR THE PROMOTION OF CHILD
HEALTH

• • •

Children are the only future of any people.
—FRANCES CRESS WELSING

• • •

We know that the outcast and misfits are the children most
likely to become violent, so it only follows that we must pull
them into the arms of love and/or acceptance, and find a place
where they fit. If our system doesn't have a place where a child
fits, there's something wrong with the system, not the child.
—WILLIAM DEFOORE

• • •

Children are the world's most valuable resource and its best
hope for the future.
—JOHN F. KENNEDY

• • •

Children

Where children are, there is the golden age.
—NOVALIS

• • •

Children are the living messages we send to a time
we will not see.
—JOHN W. WHITEHEAD

• • •

Our generation plants the trees; another gets the shade.
—CHINESE PROVERB

• • •

If you want your children to improve, let them overhear
the nice things you say about them.
—HAIM G. GINOTT

• • •

In short, the habits we form from childhood make no small difference, but rather them make all the difference.
—ARISTOTLE

• • •

My mother and I could always look outside the same window without ever seeing the same thing.
—GLORIA SWANSON

• • •

There is always a moment in childhood when the door opens and lets the future in.
—GRAHAM GREENE

• • •

Children are apt to live up to what you believe of them.
—LADY BIRD JOHNSON

• • •

The function of the child is to live his own life—not live the
life that his anxious parents think he should live.
—A.S. NEIL

• • •

The child must know that he is a miracle, that since the beginning of the world there hasn't been, and until the end of the
world will not be, another child like him.
—PABLO CASALS

• • •

To value his own good opinion, a child has to feel he is a
worthwhile person. He has to have confidence in himself as an
individual.
—SIDONIE GRUENBERG

• • •

Self-esteem is the real magic wand that can form a child's
future. A child's self-esteem affects every area of her existence,
from friends she chooses, to how well she does academically
in school, to what kind of job she gets, to even the person she
chooses to marry.
—STEPHANIE MASON

• • •

All kids need a little help, a little hope, and somebody who believes in them.
—EARVIN "MAGIC" JOHNSON

• • •

Children need love, especially when they do not deserve it.
—HAROLD HULBERT

• • •

Pretty much all of the honest truth-telling there is in the world is done by children.
—OLIVER WENDELL HOLMES

• • •

While we try to teach our children all about life, our children teach us what life is all about.
—ANGELA SCHWINDT

• • •

You can learn many things from children, how much patience
you have, for instance.
—FRANKLIN P. ADAMS

• • •

Children have never been very good at listening to their elders
but they have never failed to imitate them.
—JAMES BALDWIN

• • •

Childhood is the most beautiful of all life's seasons.
—UNKNOWN

• • •

Many things we need can wait; the child cannot. Now is the
time his bones are being formed, his blood being made, his
mind being developed. To him, we cannot say, tomorrow. His
name is today.
—GABRIELA MISTRAL

• • •

Be gentle with the young.
—JUVENAL

• • •

The best inheritance a person can give to his children is a few
minutes of his time each day.
—O.A. BATTISTA

• • •

Children have more need of models than critics.
—JOSEPH JUBERT

• • •

Children need your presence more than your presents.
—REV. JESSE JACKSON

• • •

Give love to a child, and you get a great deal back.
—JOHN RUSKIN

• • •

The child who acts unlovable is the child who most needs to be loved.
—CATHY RINDNER TEMPELSMAN

• • •

The child benefits more from being valued than evaluated.
—DON DINKMEYER

• • •

Children make you want to start life over again.
—MUHAMMAD ALI

• • •

There is a garden in every childhood, an enchanted place
where colors are brighter, the air softer, and the morning more
fragrant than ever again.
—ELIZABETH LAWRENCE

• • •

The brightest light, the light of Italy, the purest sky of Scandi-
navia in the month of June is only a half-light when one com-
pares it to the light of childhood. Even the nights were blue.
—EUGENE IONESCO

• • •

When I grow up, I want to be a little girl.
—DIANE HODGES

• • •

The older I grow the more earnestly I feel the few joys of
childhood are the best that life has to give.
—ELLEN GLASGOW

• • •

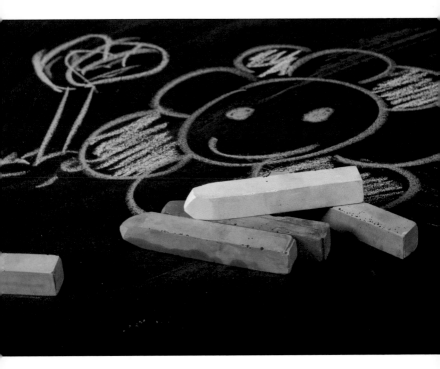

Do not handicap your children by making their lives too easy.
—ROBERT HEINLEIN

• • •

If you want children to keep their feet on the ground, put some responsibility on their shoulders.
—PAULINE PHILLIPS, "DEAR ABBY"

• • •

The more we shelter children from every disappointment, the more devastating future disappointments will be.
—FRED GOSMAN

• • •

A child building a sandcastle is not "working hard." It doesn't seem to him to be a task. It simply fills his imagination . . .
—JONATHAN MILLER

• • •

Children's games are hardly games. Children are never more
serious than when they play.
—MICHEL DE MONTAIGNE

• • •

The greatest natural resource is the minds of our children.
—WALT DISNEY

• • •

The older I get, the more I marvel at the wisdom of children.
—DAVID MORGAN

• • •

Truly wonderful the mind of a child is.
—YODA, STAR WARS

• • •

Children

Allow children to be happy in their own way, for what better
way will they find?
—SAMUEL JOHNSON

• • •

Our children are watching us live, and what we ARE shouts
louder than anything we say.
—WILFRED A. PETERSON

• • •

There are no seven wonders of the world in the eyes of a child.
There are seven million.
—WALT STREIGHTIFF

• • •

All children are artists. The problem is how to remain an artist
once he grows up.
—PABLO PICASSO

• • •

There are only two lasting bequests we can give our children.
One of these is roots; the other, wings.
—HODDING CARTER

• • •

If children grew up according to early indications, we should
have nothing but geniuses.
—JOHANN WOLFGANG VON GOETHE

• • •

There are perhaps no days of our childhood we lived so fully
as those we spent with a favorite book.
—MARCEL PROUST

• • •

One of the greatest gifts adults can give—to their offspring
and to their society—is to read to children.
—CARL SAGAN

• • •

When I was a child, my mother said to me, "If you become a soldier, you'll be a general. If you become a monk, you'll end up as the pope." Instead I became a painter and wound up as Picasso.
—PABLO PICASSO

• • •

Children are like wet cement. Whatever falls on them makes an impression.
—HAIM G. GINOTT

• • •

Nothing you do for children is ever wasted. They seem not to notice us, hovering, averting our eyes, and they seldom offer thanks, but what we do for them is never wasted.
—GARRISON KEILLOR

• • •

There are many little ways to enlarge your child's world. Love of books is best of all.
—JACQUELINE KENNEDY

• • •

Children

PART THREE

Leadership

In the battle that goes on for life
I ask for a field that is fair,
A chance that is equal with all in strife,
The courage to do and to dare.
If I should win, let it be by code,
My faith and honor held high.
If I should lose, let me stand by the road
And cheer as the winner goes by.
—KNUTE ROCKNE

• • •

Leadership is action, not position.
—DONALD H. MCGANNON

• • •

I have learned that success is to be measured not by the position that one has reached in life as by obstacles which he has overcome while trying to succeed.
—BOOKER T. WASHINGTON

• • •

An army of a thousand is easy to find, but, ah, how difficult to find a general.
—CHINESE PROVERB

• • •

We will be known forever by the tracks we leave.
—DAKOTA

• • •

The sea is so wide and my boat is so small.
—BRETON FISHERMAN'S PRAYER

• • •

Know what you want to do, hold the thought firmly, and do every day what should be done, and every sunset will see you that much nearer the goal.
—ELBERT HUBBARD

• • •

The leaders who work most effectively, it seems to me, never say "I." And that's not because they have trained themselves not to say "I." They don't think "I." They think "we"; they think "team." They understand their job to be to make the team function. They accept responsibility and don't sidestep it, but "we" gets the credit . . . This is what creates trust, what enables you to get the task done.
—PETER DRUCKER

• • •

The desire to reach for the sky runs deep in our human psyche.
—CÉSAR PELLI

• • •

Leadership is . . .
Courage to adjust mistakes,
Vision to welcome change, and
Confidence to stay out of step when everyone else is marching
to the wrong tune!
—PATTY HENDRICKSON

• • •

Some succeed because they are destined to, but most succeed
because they are determined to.
—UNKNOWN

• • •

Fairness is the art of ruffling feathers without ruining any-
body's hair-do.
—GERHARD BRONNER

• • •

Do not go where the path may lead; go instead where there is
no path and leave a trail.
—RALPH WALDO EMERSON

• • •

Leadership

Leadership

It is a rough road that leads to the heights of greatness.
—SENECA

• • •

You can't direct the wind, but you can adjust the sails.
—CHRISTOPHE POIZAT

• • •

If you don't know where you are going, any road will take you there.
—LEWIS CARROLL

• • •

A good plan is like a road map: it shows the final destination and usually the best way to get there.
—H. STANLEY JUDD

• • •

Success depends upon previous preparation, and without such
preparation there is sure to be failure.
—CONFUCIUS

• • •

When all's said and done, all roads lead to the same end. So,
it's not so much which road you take, as how you take it.
—CHARLES DE LINT

• • •

No one can persuade another to change. Each of us guards a
gate of change that can only be opened from the inside. We
cannot open the gate of another either by argument or emo-
tional appeal.
—MARILYN FERGUSON

• • •

A ship in harbor is safe—but that is not what ships are for.
—JOHN A. SHEDD

• • •

Loyalty to a petrified opinion never yet broke a chain or freed one human soul—and it never will.
—MARK TWAIN

• • •

Leaders don't force people to follow—they invite them on the journey.
—CHARLES S. LAUER

• • •

Set your sights high, the higher the better. Expect the most wonderful things to happen, not in the future, but right now. Realize that nothing is too good. Allow absolutely nothing to hamper you or hold you up in any way.
—EILEEN CADDY

• • •

Leadership is the special quality which enables people to stand up and pull the rest of us over the horizon.
—JAMES L. FISHER

• • •

To realize one's destiny is a person's only obligation . . . and when you want something, all the universe conspires in helping you to achieve it.
—PAUL COELHO

• • •

Make the most of yourself, for that is all there is of you.
—RALPH WALDO EMERSON

• • •

Whenever ideas are shared, the result is always greater than the sum of the parts.
—RICH WILLIS

• • •

Don't tell people how to do things, tell them what to do and let them surprise you with their results.
—GEORGE S. PATTON

• • •

If you're not failing every now and again, it's a sure sign that you're not trying anything innovative.
—WOODY ALLEN

• • •

What would you attempt to do if you knew you could not fail?
—ROBERT H. SCHULLER

• • •

If you get up one more time than you fall, you will make it through.
—CHINESE PROVERB

• • •

Keep your fears to yourself, but share your inspiration with others.
—ROBERT LOUIS STEVENSON

• • •

You can dream, create, design, and build the most wonderful place in the world, but it requires people to make the dream a reality.
—WALT DISNEY

• • •

If your actions inspire others to dream more, learn more, do more, and become more, you are a leader.
—JOHN QUINCY ADAMS

• • •

You do not lead by hitting people over the head—that's assault, not leadership.
—DWIGHT D. EISENHOWER

• • •

A leader takes people where they want to go. A great leader takes people where they don't necessarily want to go, but ought to be.
—ROSALYNN CARTER

• • •

My grandfather once told me that there were two kinds of people: those who do work and those who take the credit. He told me to try to be in the first group. There is much less competition.
—INDIRA GANDHI

• • •

Management is doing things right; leadership is doing the right things.
—PETER DRUCKER

• • •

The man is successful who has lived well, laughed often, and loved much; who has gained the respect of the intelligent men and the love of children; who has filled his niche and accomplished his task; who leaves the world better than he found it, whether by an improved poppy, a perfect poem, or a rescued soul; who never lacked appreciation of earth's beauty or failed to express it; who looked for the best in others and gave the best he had.
—ROBERT LOUIS STEVENSON

• • •

The only place where success comes before work is in the
dictionary.
—VIDAL SASSOON

• • •

Always do what you are afraid of doing.
—RALPH WALDO EMERSON

• • •

Whatever made you successful in the past won't work in the
future.
—LEW PLATT

• • •

Man cannot discover new oceans unless he has the courage to
lose sight of the shore.
—ANDRE GIDE

• • •

To swear off making mistakes is very easy. All you have to do is swear off having ideas.
—LEO BURNETT

• • •

The biggest job we have to teach a newly hired employee is how to fail intelligently. We have to train him to experiment over and over and to keep on trying and failing until he learns what will work.
—CHARLES F. KETTERING

• • •

Ideas won't keep; something has to be done with them.
—ALFRED NORTH WHITEHEAD

• • •

If nothing ever changed, there'd be no butterflies.
—UNKNOWN

• • •

When you have exhausted all possibilities, remember this. You
haven't.
—THOMAS EDISON

• • •

If everybody is thinking alike, then somebody isn't thinking.
—GEORGE S. PATTON

• • •

The best way to predict the future is to invent it.
—ALAN KAY

• • •

We all live under the same sky, but we don't all have the same
horizon.
—KONRAD ADENAUER

• • •

Be the change you wish the world to see.
—MAHATMA GANDHI

• • •

You will miss 100% of the shots you don't take.
—WAYNE GRETZKY

• • •

People don't care how much you know until they know how
much you care.
—JOHN C. MAXWELL

• • •

Fail to plan, plan to fail.
—CARL BUECHNER

• • •

To praise is an investment in happiness.
—GEORGE M. ADAMS

• • •

I praise loudly, I blame softly.
—CATHERINE THE GREAT

• • •

A word of encouragement during a failure is worth more than
an hour of praise after success.
—UNKNOWN

• • •

The sweetest of all sounds is praise.
—XENOPHON

• • •

The speed of the leader determines the rate of the pack.
—WAYNE LUKAS

• • •

If you refuse to accept anything but the best, you very often
get it.
—W. SOMERSET MAUGHAM

• • •

Waiting until everything is perfect before making a move is
like waiting to start a trip until all the traffic lights are green.
—KAREN IRELAND

• • •

The greater the obstacle, the more glory in overcoming it.
—MOLIÈRE

• • •

If a man does not know to what port he is steering, no wind is
favorable to him.
—SENECA

• • •

A man is a lion in his own cause.
—SCOTTISH PROVERB

• • •

Good timber does not grow with ease; the stronger the wind,
the stronger the trees.
—J. WILLARD MARRIOTT

• • •

A lion sleeps in the heart of every brave man.
—TURKISH PROVERB

• • •

PART FOUR

Human and Work Relations

We could all learn a lot from crayons:
Some are sharp,
Some are pretty,
Some are dull,
Some have weird names,
And all are different colors . . .
But they all have learned to live in the same box.
—UNKNOWN

• • •

Thousands of candles can be lit from a single candle, and the life of the candle will not be shortened. Happiness never decreases by being shared.
—BUDDHA

• • •

The door to happiness opens outward.
—UNKNOWN

• • •

It's dangerous business . . . going out your door. You step onto the road, and if you don't keep your feet, there's no knowing where you might be swept off to.
—BILBO BAGGINS,
THE FELLOWSHIP OF THE RING

• • •

Bloom where you are planted.
—MARY ENGELBREIT

• • •

I have always plucked a thistle and planted a flower where I thought a flower would grow.
—ABRAHAM LINCOLN

• • •

Always put yourself in others' shoes. If you feel it hurts, it will probably hurt the other person, too.
—UNKNOWN

• • •

Even a fish wouldn't get into trouble if it kept its mouth shut.
—KOREAN PROVERB

• • •

A good sense of humor is essential to deal with the world's
reality.
—UNKNOWN

• • •

I have seen what a laugh can do. It can transform almost
unbearable tears into something bearable, even hopeful.
—BOB HOPE

• • •

Laughter is an instant vacation.
—MILTON BERLE

• • •

Carry laughter with you wherever you go.
—HUGH SIDEY

• • •

A laugh is a smile that bursts.
—RALPH WALDO EMERSON

• • •

Laughter is the shortest distance between two people.
—VICTOR BORGE

• • •

Laughter is the tonic, the relief, the surcease for pain.
—CHARLIE CHAPLIN

• • •

A warm smile is the universal language of kindness.
—WILLIAM ARTHUR WARD

• • •

Life is short, break the rules, forgive quickly . . .
laugh uncontrollably, and never forget anything that
made you smile.
—MARK TWAIN

• • •

We shall never know all the good that a simple smile can do.
—MOTHER TERESA

• • •

Dreams are where we're going; work is how we get there.
—UNKNOWN

• • •

Let yourself be open and life will be easier. A spoon of salt in a
glass of water makes the water undrinkable. A spoon of salt in
a lake is almost unnoticed.
—BUDDHA

• • •

I find it fascinating that most people plan their vacations with better care than they plan their lives. Perhaps that is because escape is easier than change.
—JIM ROHN

• • •

Nobody can be uncheered with a balloon.
—WINNIE THE POOH

• • •

Look at everything as though you were seeing it either for the first or last time.
—BETTY SMITH

• • •

Enjoy the little things, for one day you may look back and realize they were the big things.
—ROBERT BRAULT

• • •

Think big thoughts but relish small pleasures.
—H. JACKSON BROWN, JR.

• • •

A child reminds us that playtime is an essential part of our
daily routine.
—ANONYMOUS

• • •

The shoe that fits one person pinches another; there is no
recipe for living that fits all cases.
—CARL JUNG

• • •

I learned what is obvious to a child. That life is simply a collec-
tion of little lives, each lived one day at a time. That each day
should be spent in flowers and poetry and talking to animals.
That a day spent with dreaming and sunsets and refreshing
breezes cannot be bettered.
—NICHOLAS SPARKS

• • •

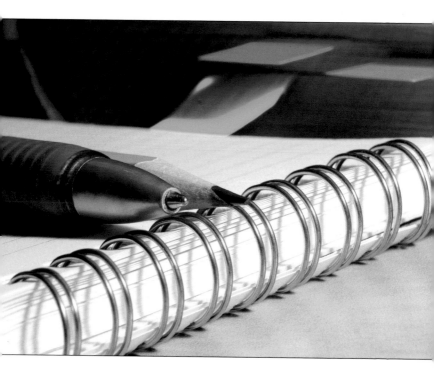

We should know that we are all part of the whole, we are all together. And everything that we do affects each other.
—YOKO ONO

• • •

Individual commitment to a group effort—that is what makes a team work, a community work, a society work, a civilization work.
—VINCE LOMBARDI

• • •

Snowflakes are one of nature's most fragile things, but just look what they can do when they stick together.
—VESTA M. KELLY

• • •

And it is still true, no matter how old you are, when you go out in the world, it is best to hold hands and stick together.
—ROBERT FULGHUM, ALL I REALLY NEED TO KNOW I LEARNED IN KINDERGARTEN

• • •

The world is full of cactus, but we don't have to sit on it.
—WILL FOLEY

• • •

Look deep into nature, and then you will understand every-thing better.
—ALBERT EINSTEIN

• • •

The only disability in life is a bad attitude.
—SCOTT HAMILTON

• • •

Don't go around saying the world owes you a living; the world owes you nothing; it was here first.
—MARK TWAIN

• • •

Never cut down a tree in the wintertime. Never make a negative decision in the low time. Never make your most important decisions when you are in your worst moods. Wait. Be patient. The storm will pass. The spring will come.
—ROBERT H. SCHULLER

• • •

When you find peace within yourself, you become the kind of person who can live at peace with others.
—PEACE PILGRIM

• • •

No one can make you feel inferior without your consent.
—ELEANOR ROOSEVELT

• • •

Wherever you go, no matter what the weather, always bring your own sunshine.
—ANTHONY J. D'ANGELO

• • •

To live through a period of stress and sorrow with another human being creates a bond which nothing seems able to break. People can be happy together and look back on their contacts very pleasantly, but such contacts will not make the same bond that sorrow lived through will create.
—ELEANOR ROOSEVELT

• • •

The world is a rose; smell and pass it on to friends.
—PERSIAN PROVERB

• • •

That is why, no matter how desperate the predicament is, I am always very much in earnest about clutching my cane, straightening my derby and fixing my tie, even though I have just landed on my head.
—CHARLIE CHAPLIN

• • •

There is more hunger for love and appreciation in this world
than for bread.
—MOTHER TERESA

• • •

One kind word can warm three winter months.
—JAPANESE PROVERB

• • •

Go confidently in the direction of your dreams. Live the life
you have always imagined.
—HENRY DAVID THOREAU

• • •

A helping word to one in trouble is often like a switch on a
railroad track . . . an inch between wreck and smooth, rolling
prosperity.
—HENRY WARD BEECHER

• • •

Praise is like sunlight to the human spirit: we cannot flower and grow without it.
—JESSE LAIR

• • •

Sticks and stones may break your bones, but words cause permanent damage.
—BARRY CHAMPLAIN

• • •

As the ocean is never full of water, so is the heart never full of love.
—UNKNOWN

• • •

You can't stand in your corner of the forest waiting for others to come to you. You have to go to them sometimes.
—WINNIE THE POOH

• • •

Love everyone as you do your dog.
—DIANE HODGES

● ● ●

True friendship is seen through the heart, not through
the eyes.
—UNKNOWN

● ● ●

The bitterest tears shed over graves are the words left unsaid
and deeds left undone.
—DUGUET

● ● ●

The first duty of love is to listen.
—PAUL TILLICH

● ● ●

Like what you do. If you don't like it, do something else.
—PAUL HARVEY

• • •

Your chances of success are directly proportional to the degree of pleasure you derive from what you do. If you are in a job you hate, face the fact squarely and get out.
—MICHAEL KORDA

• • •

If you don't get a kick out of the job you're doing, you'd better hunt for another one.
—SAMUEL VAUCLAIN

• • •

It is what we do easily and what we like to do that we do well.
—ORISON SWETT MARDEN

• • •

I never did a day's work in my life. It was all fun.
—THOMAS EDISON

• • •

Work is love made visible.
—KAHLIL GIBRAN

• • •

Find your passion and have the courage to pursue it.
—LAWRENCE BACOW

• • •

Find the seed at the bottom of your heart and bring forth a flower.
—SHIGENORI KAMEOKA

• • •

Keep a tree in your heart and perhaps a singing bird will
come.
—CHINESE PROVERB

• • •

Where flowers bloom so does hope.
—LADY BIRD JOHNSON

• • •

We need quiet time to examine our lives openly and honestly
. . . spending quiet time alone gives your mind an opportunity
to renew itself and create order.
—SUSAN L. TAYLOR

• • •

Rivers know this: there is no hurry. We shall get there
someday.
—WINNIE THE POOH

• • •

You can't stop the waves, but you can learn to surf.
—JON KABAT-ZINN

• • •

What is life?
It is the flash of a firefly in the night.
It is the breath of a buffalo in the wintertime.
It is the little shadow which runs across the grass and loses
itself in the sunset.
—CROWFOOT

• • •

The time to relax is when you don't have time for it.
—SIDNEY J. HARRIS

• • •

Sometimes our fate resembles a fruit tree in winter. Who would think that those branches would turn green again and blossom, but we hope it, we know it.
—JOHANN WOLFGANG VON GOETHE

• • •

Keep your face to the sunshine and you cannot see a shadow.
—HELEN KELLER

• • •

Live so that you wouldn't be ashamed to sell the family parrot to the town gossip.
—WILL ROGERS

• • •

Index

Index

F

Ferguson, Marilyn, 32, 146
Fisher, James L., 149
Fitzwater, Ivan Welton, 7
Foley, Will, 190
Forbes, Malcom S., 35
Ford, Henry, 40
Forester, E.M., 71
France, Anatole, 63
Franklin, Benjamin, 43, 44
Frost, Robert, 40
Fulghum, Robert, 189
Fuller, Margaret, 96

G

Gabirol, Solomon Ibn, 72
Galileo, 84
Gandhi, Indira, 157
Gandhi, Mahatma, 165
Gardner, David P., 60
Gibran, Kahlil, 107, 205
Gide, Andre, 158
Ginott, Haim G., 23, 111, 134
Glasgow, Ellen, 124
Godwin, Gail, 80
Gosman, Fred, 127
Gray, Paul E., 35
Greene, Graham, 112
Gretzky, Wayne, 165

Gross, Ronald, 40
Gruenberg, Sidonie, 115

H

Haley, William, 35
Hamilton, Scott, 190
Harris, Sidney J., 209
Harvey, Paul, 202
Hayakawa, S.I., 72
Heinlein, Robert, 127
Hendrickson, Patty, 142
Heschel, Abraham Joshua, 60
Hibben, John G., 55
Hodges, Diane, 59, 124, 201
Holmes, Oliver Wendell, 116
Holzer, Madeline Fuchs, 67
Hope, Bob, 178
Hubbard, Elbert, 68, 141
Hugo, Victor, 99
Hulbert, Harold, 116
Huxley, T.H. , 68

I

Iacocca, Lee, 16
Innan, R., 16
Ionesco, Eugene, 124

J

Jackson, Rev. Jesse, 3, 120
Johnson, Earvin "Magic", 116